UNDERSTANDING
THE BATTLE OVER
BIBLE VERSIONS

Dr. David L. Brown

Disclaimer

The author of this work has quoted the writers of many articles and books. This does not mean that the author endorses or recommends the works of others. If the author quotes someone, it does not mean that he agrees with all of the author's tenets, statements, concepts, or words, whether in the work quoted or any other work of the author. There has been no attempt to alter the meaning of the quotes; and therefore, some of the quotes are long in order to give the entire sense of the passage.

Copyright © December 2022 by David L. Brown
All Rights Reserved

Dr. David L. Brown
P. O. Box 173.
Oak Creek, WI 53154

Printed in the United States of America
REL006201: Religion: Biblical Studies - Topical

ISBN 979-8-9866583-9-1

All Scripture quotes are from the King James Bible except those verses compared and then the source is identified.

This book is an extraction of chapter 14 in Dr. Brown's larger work, "The Indestructible Book"

No part of this work may be reproduced without the expressed consent of the publisher, except for brief quotes, whether by electronic, photocopying, recording, or information storage and retrieval systems.

Address All Inquiries To:
THE OLD PATHS PUBLICATIONS, Inc.
142 Gold Flume Way
Cleveland, Georgia, 30528
U.S.A.
Web: www.theoldpathspublications.com
E-mail: TOP@theoldpathspublications.com

DEDICATION

This work is dedicated to my dear wife, Linda, who is my helper, companion, friend, and lover. For more than 53 years, she has unselfishly and joyfully set aside her own desires and done all in her power to help me be successful in everything I do. She has spent countless hours editing and proofing this work.

David L. Brown

"O taste and see that the LORD is good: blessed is the man that trusteth in him." (Psalms 34:8)

TABLE OF CONTENTS

THE PURPOSE

My purpose is to point out some of the basics relating to the battle raging over the different Bible versions so that the average Christian in the pew can understand what is going on and why they should use the King James Bible.

INTRODUCTORY THOUGHTS

The Bible is the foundation of literally everything in New Testament Christianity! Therefore, it is imperative that you have an uncorrupted Bible. If something does not have a biblical base, it should be rejected. We read in **1 Thessalonians 5:21**:

> ***Prove all things; hold fast that which is good.***

The English word **prove** is a translation of the Greek word δοκιμαζετε – dokimazete (*dok-im-ad'zate*). The word carries the idea of **proving a thing whether it is worthy or not**. So, the question is, "How are we to go about **proving** something?" I believe **Isaiah 8:20** gives us insight into the answer to this question –

> ***"To the law and to the testimony: <u>if they speak not according to this word</u>, it is because there is no light in them."***

In other words, **examine everything by the words of the Bible** and if it does not line up, reject it!

Friends, the Bible, **our King James Bible, is the "GOLD STANDARD" for EVERY THING in the** Christian life! 2 Timothy 3:16-17 says:

> ***"All scripture is given by inspiration of God, and is profitable for doctrine, for***

> *reproof, for correction, for instruction in righteousness: 17 That the man of God may be perfect, thoroughly furnished unto all good works.*"

As I have often said – The Bible tells us what's right, what's not right, how to get right and how to stay right.

Since THE BIBLE IS SO IMPORTANT, it should come as no surprise that the true Words of God, as found in our King James Bible, are under attack by our adversary, the Devil, who has transformed himself into an angel of light and his ministers into ministers of righteousness (**2 Corinthians 11:14-15**).

CHAPTER 1

UNDERSTANDING THE BATTLE TERMINOLOGY

In order to understand the Battle over Bible versions, you first need to understand some of ***the battle vocabulary***. Both sides in the Bible version battle toss around these unfamiliar words, and if you do not really understand the *vocabulary*, it is hard to understand exactly what the issues are.

DEFINITIONS

Let's look at and define some of the key words.

Autographs – An autograph is the original texts (of the Bible) that were written either by the hand of the author or by a scribe under the supervision of the author. For centuries there have been NO Hebrew or Aramaic **autographs** of any Old Testament book or passage. There were none in Jesus' day. Nor are there any Greek **autographs** of any New Testament Book or portion thereof. No one has ever seen one, since probably about 150 A.D.

Apographs – A handwritten copy of the original. There are thousands of **apographs** still extant today.

Manuscripts – All Bibles were hand copied; written by scribes onto parchment, vellum, papyrus or paper prior to the printing of the Gutenberg Bible (also called the 42 line Bible & Mazarin Bible) which was printed on a printing press using moveable type in 1454-1455.

THERE ARE FOUR KINDS OF GREEK MANUSCRIPTS

There are **four kinds of Greek manuscripts** that we have in our possession today:

1) **papyri,**
2) **uncials,**
3) **cursives, and**
4) **lectionaries.**

"The Greek manuscripts of the New Testament, so far as known, were written on papyrus, parchment, or paper. The *autographs*, both of the historical and epistolary writers, are supposed to have been written on papyrus. The great uncials copies and the most valued of the minuscules and lectionaries were written on parchment, while paper was employed largely in the making of the later lectionaries and the printed texts of the New Testament." (*Praxis In Manuscripts of the Greek New Testament* by Rev. Charles F. Sitterly; 1898; p.15).

NEW TESTAMENT PAPYRI MANUSCRIPTS

For a listing see - www.kchanson.com/papyri.html#NTP

Papyrus is a brittle kind of paper made out of the papyrus plant, which grows in Egypt. To my knowledge there are about <u>123 papyrus fragment manuscripts of the New Testament</u>.

See - http://en.wikipedia.org/wiki/List_of_New_Testament_papyri.

Most of those surviving early texts only have a few verses on them. The most ancient example is the John Ryland papyrus fragment p52 (*p* stands for papyrus) which includes portions of **John 18:31-33 & 37-38**. It is housed in John Ryland University Library in Manchester, England. The fragment is believed to have been written sometime around 150 A.D.

There are **6 papyri** that I am aware of, which record large portions of the New Testament. P45, dated around 200 A.D., contains portions of all **four Gospels and Acts**. P46, from the second century, has almost all of **Paul's epistles and Hebrews**. P47, also from the second-century, contains **Revelation 9-17**. These are from what is called the Beatty Papyri housed in Dublin Castle in Dublin, Ireland. Then there are three lengthy papyri from the Bodmer Papyri. P66 is a second century papyrus that contains almost all of **John**. P72, a third or fourth century papyrus, contains all of **1 and 2 Peter and Jude**. Finally, P75, dated between 175-200 A.D., contains most of **Luke through John 15**.

THE UNCIALS OR MAJUSCULE MANUSCRIPTS

See list at – www.en.wikipedia.org/wiki/List_of_New_Testament_uncials

Uncial comes from the Latin word **_uncialis_**, which means inch-high. It is used to delineate a type of Greek and Latin writing which features capital letters. There are few, if any, divisions between words in uncial manuscripts and no punctuation to speak of. The word majuscule, meaning large or capital letter, is a synonym for uncial. There are about **290 uncial manuscripts** of all text types.

Three of the most famous uncial New Testament manuscripts are the **_Sinaiticus_** (also called by the first letter of the Hebrew alphabet a – Aleph) believed to have been written about 350 A.D. Then there is **_Vaticanus_** (also called "**B**"), believed to have been written about 350 A.D. Then there is **Codex Alexandrinus**, (identified as "**A**"), written about 450 A.D.

Speakers on the Bible versions' issue will often refer to the manuscripts using the uncial letter designations, instead of their longer names.

CURSIVE OR MINUSCULE MANUSCRIPTS

Cursive or minuscule manuscripts are Greek manuscripts written in lower case letters, more like handwriting. The letters flow together, much like writing of today. There are spaces between words and some degree of punctuation. At last count there are 2,764 cursive Greek manuscripts.

See list at www.biblebelievers.net/BibleVersions/kjcforv5.htm#XXIV

LECTIONARY MANUSCRIPTS

The word **lection** comes from a Latin root word meaning **"to read."** Lectionaries are portions of Scriptures in Greek (or Latin) Bibles that were read in the church services during the year. There are at least 2,882 known lectionaries in existence.

See www.csntm.org/Manuscripts.aspx

When you add up all the figures, **there are about 6059** Greek manuscripts in existence today for the New Testament. Another source says, "The New Testament has been preserved in more manuscripts than any other ancient work, having over 5,400 (now more than 6,000) complete or fragmented Greek manuscripts, 10,000 Latin manuscripts and 9,300 manuscripts in various other ancient languages including Syriac, Slavic, Gothic, Ethiopic, Coptic and Armenian. The dates of these manuscripts range from

the 2nd century up to the invention of the printing press in the 15th century."
See - en.wikipedia.org/wiki/Biblical_manuscript.

What you need to know about these 6,000 plus manuscripts and portions is that there are only about 45 to 50 Greek manuscripts that support the type of Greek text that underlies the modern versions of the Bible, but there are 5,000 plus that support the Textus Receptus type text that underlies our King James Bible. Figure it out. Figure it out! About 99% of all the manuscript evidence supports the text type from which the King James Bible is translated.

OTHER WORDS AND PHRASES THAT RELATE TO THE BIBLE VERSION BATTLE
INSPIRATION

The word *inspiration* is derived from the Greek word ψεοπνευστοϖ-<u>theopneutos</u> (**2 Timothy 3:16**), which literally means "**God breathed**" or more accurately, "**breathed into by God.**" Charles Ryrie writes that inspiration is – "God's superintending of human authors so that, using their own individual personalities, they composed and recorded <u>without error</u> in the words of the original autographs His revelation to man."

Dr. Thomas Strouse puts it this way – "Inspiration is the process whereby the Holy Spirit led the writers of Scripture to record accurately His very words; the product of the process was an inspired original." (Dr. Thomas Strouse, Dean Emmanuel Baptist Theological Seminary; *The Translation Model Predicated by Scripture* – by way of *The Attack On The Canon of Scripture* by Dr. H. D. Williams; p. 13).

There is an important fact you must know when it comes to biblical inspiration. It was the WORDS that were inspired, not the men! God worked through the men by His Holy Spirit with the result of the WORDS being inspired. That is what **2 Peter 1:20-21** is saying:

> **"Knowing this first, that no prophecy of the scripture is of any private interpretation. 21 For the prophecy came not in old time by the will of man: but holy men of God spake as they were moved by the Holy Ghost."**

Let me explain what is being said in **verse 21**. The idea is that Scripture neither proceeds from the prophet's own knowledge, thoughts, ideas or inventions, nor was it rooted in the calculation or conjecture of the one to whom it was revealed. As one commentator put it, **"this means that the origin of the Scripture was not of anyone's private or personal ideas."**

VERBAL-PLENARY INSPIRATION

I believe the Bible teaches **verbal-plenary inspiration.**

PLENARY INSPIRATION

Let me first explain the term *"plenary"* as it relates to inspiration. It simply means **"full, complete, entire."** The Bible is equally inspired from Genesis to Revelation. Generally, the term is employed to emphasize that all of the respective components of the Scriptures were given by God. This means that the Bible's historical depictions are true, that incidental scientific references are factual as well, and, in a word, that all biblical documents are completely accurate. **Psalms 119:160** is an example of a passage that teaches *plenary inspiration* –

> *"Thy word is true from the beginning: and every one of thy righteous judgments endureth for ever."*

VERBAL INSPIRATION (THE BIBLICAL VIEW OF INSPIRATION)

What does **Verbal Inspiration** mean? This means that the <u>words</u> are divinely inspired and that **every word of the Bible**, as it was originally written, is from God.

The theological explanation of inspiration says that the Holy Spirit guided chosen servants of God <u>in the choice of the very words</u> they used. They retained the proper use of their powers and faculties, yet were guided or assisted to use such language as would convey the mind of the Spirit in its full and unimpaired integrity. Again, <u>this verbal inspiration was of the original autographs alone.</u>

A. A. Hodge put it this way, "It is meant that the divine influence, of whatever kind it may have been, which accompanied the sacred writers in what they wrote, extends to their expression of their thoughts in language, as well as to the thoughts themselves. The effect being that in the original autograph copies the language expresses the thought God intended to convey with infallible accuracy, so that the words as well as the thoughts are God's revelation to us."

Does the Bible teach the concept of **verbal inspiration**? YES! We already looked at **2 Peter 1:20-21**. Another key passage that I mentioned earlier is **2 Timothy 3:16-17**:

> ***<u>All scripture is given by inspiration of God</u>, and is profitable for doctrine, for reproof, for correction, for instruction in righteousness: 17 That the man of God may be perfect, thoroughly furnished unto all good works.***"

In fact, the Bible contains hundreds of passages in which the authors claim divine inspiration for their message. Also, there are direct accounts of written revelation. One illustration is Moses receiving the Ten Commandments! The phrase, ***"the word of the LORD came..."*** occurs 92 times in the King James

Bible and another 19 times we read the phrase, *"the words of the Lord."* The phrase, *"thus saith the Lord..."* occurs 415 times as well. In the Bible we have the Word and the Words of God.

Paul makes a most striking contrast between man's word on the one hand, and God's Word on the other in **1 Thessalonians 2:13:**

> *"For this cause also thank we God without ceasing, because, when ye received the word of God which ye heard of us, ye received it not as the word of men, but as it is in truth, the word of God, which effectually worketh also in you that believe."*

So, as we have in our church doctrinal statement – "The process of God's breathing out His Words occurred only once when He breathed out or 'inspired' the Hebrew, Aramaic and Greek texts. Though the process of inspiration has never been repeated, the product of inspiration, that is, the Hebrew, Aramaic, and Greek Words, have been preserved by God in the Words of the Masoretic Hebrew and Textus Receptus Greek that underlie the King James Bible."

THOUGHT-CONCEPT INSPIRATION (THE COUNTERFEIT VIEW OF INSPIRATION)

Doesn't everyone believe in verbal-plenary inspiration? NO! An increasing number of churches,

Bible Colleges and seminaries teach that God gave the thoughts BUT NOT THE SPECIFIC WORDS OF SCRIPTURE! Dr. Thomas Strouse explains the ***thought-concept*** theory this way, "They believe God inspired His divine concepts and then preserved these concepts in the extant Manuscripts (MSS)." He goes on to say, "Since the concepts are inspired and preserved, the exact words representing these concepts may not be available and may vary." He further notes that the textual critics suggest that, "through the science of textual criticism, man can restore the approximate wording of the original text."
(The Biblical Defense For The Verbal, Plenary Preservation of God's Word by Dr. T. M. Strouse; www.graceway.com/articles/articles_007.htm)

In fact, ***textual criticism*** is <u>**not a science at all**</u>! It is the contrived invention of unsaved men!

One commentator gives an illustration of how ***thought-concept*** inspiration works. "When Paul wrote **1 Corinthians 13** the only thing God gave was <u>some general thoughts</u> on the subject of love. The words of the text we owe to Paul." (*Is the Bible Reliable? Our God-Breathed Bible;* John MacArthur; Tape GC 1343).

That's wrong. In **1 Corinthians 2:13,** Paul shows unmistakably that <u>divine inspiration pertains also to the **words**</u> and <u>not merely to the thought,</u> saying:

> *"Which things also we speak, not in __the words__ which man's wisdom teacheth, but which the Holy Ghost teacheth."*

Nearly all the "New Versions" come from the thought-conceptual view of inspiration. They deny God inspired His Words. The main point that needs to be made clear is that there is NO PLACE in the Bible that teaches mere thought-concept inspiration. It is a humanly devised invention that is engineered by the Devil!

PROVIDENTIAL PRESERVATION

I hold to the position of Dr. Edward F. Hills (1912-1981) who stated that the Scriptures have been preserved by God in His providence so that the Church would always have the Words as *a light to her feet and a lamp to her path.* (*The Providential Preservation of The Greek Text of The New Testament;* Fourth edition 1983; by Rev. W. MacLean, M.A.).

This is NOT a unique position! In 1649 the Protestant Reformers in their Westminster Confession of Faith stated – "The Old Testament in Hebrew (which was the native language of the people of God of old), and the New Testament in Greek (which at the time of the writing of it was most generally known to the nations), being immediately inspired by God, and <u>by His singular care and providence kept pure in all ages,</u>

are therefore authentical; so as in all controversies of religion the Church is finally to appeal unto them."

Many people are saying today that God abandoned His Hebrew, Aramaic and Greek Words rather than preserving them. The great defender of the Traditional Text and our King James Bible, Dean John Burgon disagreed. He wrote in his work, *The Traditional Text,* "There exists no reason for supposing that the Divine Agent, who in the first instance thus gave to mankind the Scriptures of Truth, straightway abdicated His office; took no further care of His work; abandoned those precious writings to their fate."

One preacher put it very well in an evening sermon I heard – "God gave us His original Words by verbal-plenary inspiration. God preserved those Words by verbal-plenary preservation. Almighty God promised and performed both events." What he said is true! The Bible teaches not only the verbal-plenary inspiration of the original autographs, but also the verbal-plenary preservation of those autographs. The verbal-plenary inspiration for the original autographs of the Bible would be absolutely useless without the providential, verbal-plenary preservation of those Words! Why? Because nobody for 1,800 years or more has ever seen any portion of any book from the original books (autographs) of the Bible. If no one has ever seen the originals, how could they ever know or live by the

Words of God? In fact, **the Lord Jesus Christ taught the preservation of the Scriptures**.

Matthew 4:4 says:

> **"But he answered and said, It is written, Man shall not live by bread alone, but by every word that proceedeth out of the mouth of God."**

The phrase **"every word"** in the Greek is *panti rhmati* which means **each and every word**. Christ here is quoting the last portion of **Deuteronomy 8:3**. He clearly believed it had been preserved because if we are to live by *"every word that proceedeth out of the mouth of God"* we must know what those words are.

I remind you that there were NO original Old Testament autographs in Christ's day, yet He believed the Words of God had been preserved because He authoritatively quoted them.

Our Lord affirms biblical preservation in **Matthew 5:18** when he said:

> **"For verily I say unto you, Till heaven and earth pass, one jot or one tittle shall in no wise pass from the law, till all be fulfilled."**

Then there are His words recorded in **Luke 16:17**:

> ***"And it is easier for heaven and earth to pass, than one tittle of the law to fail."***

Here He affirms that the Scriptures are more stable than Heaven and Earth!

Our Lord affirms the preservation of His words in all three Gospels:

> ***Matthew 24:35 "Heaven and earth shall pass away, but <u>my words shall not pass away</u>.***" (See also Mark 13:31 & Luke 21:33).

There is one final passage I want to point out:

> ***Matthew 5:18 "For verily I say unto you, Till heaven and earth pass, one jot or one tittle shall in no wise pass from the law, till all be fulfilled."***

Jesus is reinforcing the accuracy of the Scriptures down to the smallest detail and the slightest punctuation mark - because they are the VERY WORDS OF GOD.

Perhaps the strongest verses affirming the providential preservation of the Bible are:

> ***Psalms 12:6-7 "The words of the LORD are pure words: as silver tried in a furnace of earth, purified seven times. 7 Thou shalt keep them, O***

> ***LORD, thou shalt preserve them from this generation for ever."***

I will conclude with this statement – "The providential preservation of the Scriptures is also a necessary consequence of their divine inspiration. The God who inspired the Scriptures and gave them to His people to be an authoritative guide and consolation cannot allow this perfect and final revelation of His will to perish. Because God has inspired the Scriptures, He has also preserved them by His providence." (*The King James Version Defended* by Edward F. Hills).

FORMAL EQUIVALENCY OR LITERAL TRANSLATION

William Tyndale gave us the first printed English New Testament in 1526. He had a holy fear of God and reverence for His Word. In October of 1536 he was martyred for his faith and for printing a Bible in English for the people to read. Regarding his translation of the New Testament he wrote – "I call God to record against the day we shall appear before our Lord Jesus, to give a reckoning of our doings, that I never altered one syllable of God's Word against my conscience, nor would [I so alter it] this day, if all that is in the earth, whether it be pleasure, honor, or riches, might be given me." Tyndale gave us a formal equivalent translation of the New Testament from the Traditional Text or Textus Receptus.

Why was William Tyndale so cautious in his Bible translating? Look at these verses –

Deuteronomy 4:1-2 "Now therefore hearken, O Israel, unto the statutes and unto the judgments, which I teach you, for to do them, that ye may live, and go in and possess the land which the LORD God of your fathers giveth you. 2 Ye shall not add unto the word which I command you, neither shall ye diminish ought from it, that ye may keep the commandments of the LORD your God which I command you."

Proverbs 30:5-6 "Every word of God is pure: he is a shield unto them that put their trust in him. 6 Add thou not unto his words, lest he reprove thee, and thou be found a liar."

Revelation 22:18-19 "For I testify unto every man that heareth the words of the prophecy of this book, If any man shall add unto these things, God shall add unto him the plagues that are written in this book: 19 And if any man shall take away from the words of the book of this prophecy, God shall take away his part out of the book of life, and out of the holy city, and from the things which are written in this book."

Now to the definition of **Formal Equivalency**: It refers to the method of translating by finding reasonably equivalent words and phrases while following the **forms** of the source language as closely as possible. It is often referred to as "**literal translation**." It is a literal translation, (formal equivalent translation), when, as closely as possible, the Bible is translated *word-for-word*. If the original has a noun, then a noun is used in the translation.

A formal equivalent translation of the Bible is the best method that can be used in translating from the Hebrew, Aramaic and Greek underlying texts. But the underlying text that you translate from must be the Hebrew Masoretic text of the Old Testament and the Textus Receptus in the New Testament.

Let me explain why I say that it is the BEST way of translating the Bible. The Psalmist declared:

> *"Forever, O Lord, thy word is settled in heaven." Psalm 119:89.*

You might say, the MASTER COPY of the Word of God is in Heaven. Our Lord Jesus Christ declared:

> *"Heaven and earth shall pass away, but my words shall not pass away." Matthew 24:35. Again He said, "For verily I say unto you, Till heaven and earth pass, one jot or one tittle shall in no wise pass from the law, till all be fulfilled." Matthew 5:18.*

What is a **jot**? The word "**jot**" is the translation of the Hebrew word "**Yodh.**"

This is a Hebrew ׳ Yodh , which is the 10th letter of the Hebrew alphabet. It is also the smallest letter of the Hebrew alphabet.

What is a **tittle**? Dr. Thomas Strouse believes that tittle literally means a dot. He says, "Tittle is the specifically accurate English word for a dot, coming through the German from the Hebrew for dot or teat."
(Taken from an article, Luke 16:17—One Tittle by Dr. Thomas Strouse, http://www.deanburgonsociety.org/Preservation/tittle.htm).

Why am I explaining this to you? Simply this: Since our Lord Jesus was concerned about the smallest pen stroke of the smallest letter in the Hebrew text, it should also be important to us that we use a Bible translation that is based on **formal equivalency**, using the BEST TEXT GROUP (<u>which is the Received Text</u>). **Our King James Bible is the best formal equivalent translation of the right text group**. There is none better.

A formal equivalent translation lets the reader interpret for himself. And that is exactly what believers are to do. **2 Timothy 2:15:**

> *"Study to show thyself approved unto God, a workman that needeth not to be ashamed, rightly dividing the word of truth."*

DYNAMIC EQUIVALENCE OR FUNCTIONAL EQUIVALENCE

This attitude of fear and trembling toward God's holy Word does not exist among most all of the present-day Bible translators. They are not afraid of <u>adding to</u>, <u>subtracting from</u> and <u>changing</u> the eternal Word of God.

Dynamic Equivalence, also called **Functional Equivalence**, is a translation method in which the translator attempts to reflect the thought of the writer in the source language rather than the words and forms. It is not so concerned about the grammatical *form* of the original language as it is with getting across the *thoughts*. DYNAMIC EQUIVALENCE AIMS TO TRANSLATE THOUGHTS RATHER THAN WORDS. However, the BIG problem is, a dynamic equivalence translation is more interpretive. And because it is more interpretive, the translators do not always know whether their interpretation is right. In essence, when dynamic equivalency is used, the translators put their own spin on the Bible!

Here are some actual illustrations where this type of translation has been used. From the KJB, look at **Isaiah 1:18:**

"Come now, and let us reason together, saith the LORD: though your sins be as scarlet, they shall be <u>as white as snow</u>; though they be red like crimson, they shall be as wool."

David Cloud relates this in reference to this passage – "An example of adapting the Bible's language to today's cultural situations (using dynamic equivalency) was related to me by the head of the Bible Society in Nepal. He told of one of the projects of the United Bible Societies, which was done in a part of the world in which the <u>people had not seen snow</u>. The translators, therefore, decided to translate Isaiah 1:18—"...though your sins be as scarlet, they shall be <u>white as the inside of a coconut</u>....""

Cloud goes on – "Consider some other examples of the way these versions change the Word of God to conform with culture. The following illustrations were given to us by Ross Hodsdon of Bibles International, formerly with Wycliffe:

In a translation for Eskimos in Alaska, '<u>lamb</u>' was replaced with '<u>seal pup</u>.'

In a translation in the Makusi language of Brazil, '<u>son of man</u>' was replaced with '<u>older brother</u>.'

In another Wycliffe translation '<u>fig tree</u>' was replaced with '<u>banana tree</u>.'"

That is NOT what God said! That is tampering with the Words of God! THAT IS WRONG. When one departs from the principle of a literal translation, the mind of the translator and the culture and understanding of the people become the authority rather than God's actual Words.

The same thing is happening in the modern versions today, because they are using the dynamic equivalent translation model. They are translating thoughts and not the Words of God.

PARAPHRASE

A **paraphrase** is a very, very loose translation of the Bible. In a paraphrase, the translator is neither concerned about translating the exact words, nor even the exact meaning of the original text. In fact, a paraphrase is a retelling of something in your own words. A paraphrase of the Bible is different from a translation. It is like a condensed commentary where the one that is doing the paraphrasing does no translating but retells what is in the Bible in his own words, paying little or no attention to the exact words of the Bible. In reality, a paraphrase is not a Bible at all. It is the author's explanation of the Bible in his own words. Some popular Paraphrase Bibles are – The Living Bible; The New Living Bible, Good News for Modern Man; The Good News Bible, The Message; The

Amplified Bible; The Clear Word Bible, etc. ***NOTE***: **A paraphrase Bible is not really a Bible at all.**

I affirm once again: the King James Bible is the best Bible in the English language.

HIGHER CRITICISM

The phrase, ***Higher Criticism***, was coined in 1778 by Johann Gottfried Eichhorn who lived from 1752 to 1827. It originally referred to the work of liberal German Biblical scholars, under the leadership of Ferdinand Christian Baur of the Tübingen School, of the University of Tübingen, located in the city of that name in Germany. The phrase **"higher criticism"** became popular in Europe (and England) from the mid-18th century.

SO WHAT IS "HIGHER CRITICISM"?

Higher criticism treats the Bible as a text created by human beings at a particular historical time and for various human motives. "They based their interpretations on a presupposition that the Bible is not divinely inspired and that a conglomerate of unknown authors and editors assembled and modified the Bible as they desired." (www.foundationsforfreedom.net/Topics/Bible/Bible_Reliability.html).

Higher critics question the historical reliability of the Bible, biblical Creation, a real Adam and Eve, Noah, the Ark and the global flood, the miracles recorded in the Bible, the virgin birth of Christ, the literal, physical, bodily resurrection of Christ and more.

Let me give you an illustration. In the 1771 first edition of the Encyclopedia Britannica the editors treated the account of Noah and the Ark as essentially factual, and even offered some scientific calculations demonstrating that the animals could fit on the Ark. Why? Because they considered the Bible to be the Word of God. All that changed by the 8th edition (1852) of the Encyclopedia Britannica. The facts of Noah and the Ark were questioned. Why? It is because the editorial staff had been infected by **higher criticism,** and had adopted the position of the "learned" biblical scholars who did not believe in the inspiration of the Bible.

Now, I will share some illustrations relating specifically to the Bible. "**Higher criticism** has questioned the authenticity of history as the Bible presents it. Higher critics would deny the historicity of Israel's Exodus out of Egypt. With such presumptions, they strongly suggest that the Book of Exodus was just a story written later on to provide the people of Israel a national identity." (www.foundationsforfreedom.net/Topics/Bible/Bible_Reliability.html).

Another illustration relates to the assertion of *higher critics* who claimed that Isaiah 53 was inserted into the Old Testament book of Isaiah after the

<u>time of Jesus</u>. However, with the discovery of the Dead Sea Scrolls, particularly the scroll of Isaiah, which was dated to 335-324 B.C., **it proves that Isaiah 53 was NOT an insertion!**

Previous to the discovery of the Dead Sea Scroll of Isaiah, the oldest scroll of the Old Testament dated to about 900 A.D. Obviously, with the discovery of this older scroll, Isaiah 53 could no longer be said to have been inserted after Jesus' time. The higher critics were shown to be liars!

However, ***higher criticism*** certainly has done great damage to belief in the Bible because the result of their calling into question the events of the Bible was that the average person who heard these theories postulated by so-called ***"Bible scholars,"*** stated as facts, was that many of them became disillusioned with the Bible. Christian friends, this higher critical view of the Bible is still alive and well today. You see it being promoted on TV, in modern publication and on the Internet.

Bible believers reject the **higher critical** approach to the Bible! We believe the Bible IS the inspired, inerrant, infallible Word of God. We believe such verses as – **Psalm 119:160** *"Thy word is true from the beginning: and every one of thy righteous judgments endureth for ever."* We believe **2 Timothy**

3:16 which says, *"All scripture is given by inspiration of God, and is profitable for doctrine, for reproof, for correction, for instruction in righteousness."*

CHAPTER 2
TEXTUAL CRITICISM

Textual criticism is a humanly contrived method that so-called "Bible scholars" use to discover what the original manuscripts of the Bible most likely said. <u>The object of textual criticism is to restore, as nearly as possible, the original text of a work, the autograph of which has been lost</u>. That is why they have produced numerous editions of the ***critical text* of the Greek New Testament**. They are seeking to restore it but still have not accomplished the job.

The 24th edition of Nestle-Aland Greek New Testament says in the front –

Novum Testamentum Graece seeks to provide the reader with the critical appreciation of the whole textual tradition... It should naturally be understood that <u>this text is a working text</u> (in the sense of the century-long Nestle tradition); <u>it is not to be considered as definitive</u>, but as <u>a stimulus to further efforts towards redefining and verifying the text of the New Testament</u>.

So, how do the editors of these critical Greek New Testaments determine how they make the changes as they go about restoring the New Testament? I think you will be shocked! For the answer we need to look at the 27th edition of the *Novum Testamentum Graece* edited by Kurt Aland and Barbara Aland (27th edition, Stuttgart, 1993). It was agreed upon by the committee as the "best" reading and it has nothing to do with the "original" text. When they disagreed on the best reading to print, they voted. Who voted? Barbara Aland, Kurt Aland, Johannes Karavidopoulos, Cardinal Carlo M. Martini, and Bruce Metzger.

Now, the reason I am explaining this rather technical information is because it is ***the critical text of the New Testament from which nearly all the modern versions of the Bible are translated***. And let me tell you this. If the text the modern Bible translators use for their bibles "**is not to be considered as definitive**" then certainly their translation cannot be considered definitive.

This bogus assertion, that the original readings of the Bible, particularly the New Testament, have been altered or lost and need to be restored, is a major battlefront in the war over Bible versions. **I reject this critical view of the Bible** based on the promises that God has given us in the Bible. **God has preserved His Word and Words**. Those words are in the Hebrew Masoretic text of the Old Testament and the Greek Textus Receptus of our New Testament. As I said previously, I align myself with Dean John William

Burgon who said, "If you and I believe that the original writings of the Scriptures were verbally inspired by God, then of necessity they must have been providentially preserved through the ages."

Though I have rehearsed many of these verses earlier in this book, I will do it again so that you will believe God that He has preserved His Words, and we can read those preserved words in our King James Bible.

- *Psalms 12:6-7 "The words of the LORD are pure words: as silver tried in a furnace of earth, purified seven times. 7 Thou shalt keep them, O LORD, thou shalt preserve them from this generation for ever."*

- *Psalms 33:11 "The counsel of the LORD standeth for ever, the thoughts of his heart to all generations."*

- *Psalms 100:5 "For the LORD is good; his mercy is everlasting; and his truth endureth to all generations."*

- *Psalms 111:7-8 "The works of his hands are verity and judgment; all his commandments are sure. 8 They stand fast for ever and ever, and are done in truth and uprightness."*

- *Psalms 117:2 "For his merciful kindness is great toward us: and the truth of the*

LORD endureth for ever. Praise ye the LORD."

- *Psalms 119:152 "Concerning thy testimonies, I have known of old that thou hast founded them for ever."*

- *Psalms 119:160 "Thy word is true from the beginning: and every one of thy righteous judgments endureth for ever."*

- *Isaiah 40:8 "The grass withereth, the flower fadeth: but the word of our God shall stand for ever."*

- *Isaiah 59:21 "As for me, this is my covenant with them, saith the LORD; My spirit that is upon thee, and my words which I have put in thy mouth, shall not depart out of thy mouth, nor out of the mouth of thy seed, nor out of the mouth of thy seed's seed, saith the LORD, from henceforth and for ever."*

- *Matthew 24:35 "Heaven and earth shall pass away, but my words shall not pass away."*

- *John 10:35 "...the scripture cannot be broken."*

- *1 Peter 1:23-25 "Being born again, not of corruptible seed, but of incorruptible, by the word of God, which liveth and abideth for ever. 24 For all flesh is as grass, and all the glory of man as the flower of grass. The grass withereth, and the flower thereof falleth away: 25 But the word of the Lord endureth for ever. And this is the word which by the gospel is preached unto you."*

CHAPTER 3

THE CORRUPTION OF THE NEW TESTAMENT TEXT

Before we forge ahead, I want to review several important terms – ***Higher criticism*** is a philosophy that rejects the inspiration of the Bible and treats the Bible as a text created by different people. ***Textual criticism*** is the theory that the <u>text of the true words of the New Testament had been lost</u> by the end of the 3rd century and it may or may not be recoverable. They believe that the New Testament remained in a corrupted state for more than 1500 years and that only in the late 19th century, through ***textual criticism***, was the process of reconstructing the true text of the New Testament even started. This reconstructed Greek New Testament is called the ***Critical Text,*** because it was reconstructed using the humanly contrived principles of ***textual criticism***. This ever-evolving ***Critical Text*** is based on early corrupted manuscripts. ***Critical scholars*** do not believe that the New Testament has been completely reconstructed, but is only in the process of being reconstructed. Therefore, no one knows for sure what it really says, because it is ever changing. There are 27 editions of the Nestle-Aland Greek Critical Text New Testament; each edition changes words in numerous places.

However, there is a **BIG PROBLEM** with the theory of *textual criticism*. **It is a man-made lie!** The same God who inspired the Bible has also preserved the Bible. Let me share with you <u>two additional verses</u> that teach Bible preservation...

- ***Isaiah 40:8 "The grass withereth, the flower fadeth: but <u>the word of our God shall stand for ever.</u>"***

- ***Isaiah 59:21 "As for me, this is my covenant with them, saith the LORD; My spirit that is upon thee, and my words which I have put in thy mouth, shall not depart out of thy mouth, nor out of the mouth of thy seed, nor out of the mouth of thy seed's seed, saith the LORD, from henceforth and for ever."***

When we read the phrase *"shall not depart out of thy mouth..."* that means **God's Words will continue** so you can quote it yourself, for your children, for your grandchildren and succeeding generations forever!

What I am saying is this. There is a **<u>preserved line</u>** of Hebrew, Aramaic and Greek texts: the ones that underlie our King James Bible. But there is a **<u>corrupted line of texts</u>** also. This corrupt text line is the one from which nearly ALL of the New Translations come.

THE EARLY CORRUPTION OF THE NEW TESTAMENT

While I have shared some of this material earlier in the book, I want to go over it again, since it is so important. Purposeful efforts to alter and corrupt the New Testament began almost immediately after the Gospels and epistles (letters) were written. This is affirmed by Paul in **2 Corinthians 2:17:**

> *"For we are not as many, <u>which</u> <u>corrupt the word of God</u>: but as of sincerity, but as of God, in the sight of God speak we in Christ."*

The word, **corrupt,** is a translation of the Greek word καπηλευοντεϖ – kapaleuontes (kap-ale-loo-entace) which means a **huckster**. <u>A **huckster** is a shrewd, aggressive salesman who is less than honest.</u> One scholar said this about the word – The Greek word was used to describe shady "wine-dealers *playing tricks with their wines*; mixing the new, harsh wines, so as to make them pass for old. They not only sold their wares in the market, but had *wine-shops* all over the town..." where they peddled their corrupt wine claiming it was genuine. They made a bundle of money by their deception.

So, <u>how is this word [**huckster**] used in reference to the Word of God</u>? Gnostic hucksters, and other enemies of Christianity, took the pure Words of God and, like the shady wine dealers, mixed in their own philosophies, opinions and ideas, and then peddled it as the real thing.

Let me illustrate just how Gnostics corrupted the Alexandrian line of New Testament texts. Consider Marcion. He was **born** between 85 to 110 A.D. No one knows for sure. He founded his own Gnostic-oriented heretical sect in about 144 A.D. He taught that the God of the Old Testament could not have been the Father of Jesus Christ, because Christ speaks of His Father as a God of love, but the God of the Jews was a God of wrath. Marcion taught that Jehovah, the God of the Old Testament, created the world, but that all created flesh was evil. Further, he taught that the soul/spirit of man was created by a greater god, one who was above Jehovah. <u>This greater god created the spiritual realm and was the true Father of Jesus Christ</u>. To release man's soul from his flesh, this greater god sent Christ. Christ appeared, in the form of a thirty-year-old man, <u>in a spiritual body that appeared to be physical but was not a physical body</u>. **Salvation,** he taught, **was gained by renouncing Jehovah and all things physical**. Marcion rejected the Hebrew Scriptures, and the quotations of those Hebrew Scriptures in the New Testament. **The followers of Marcion issued their own New Testament composed of Luke and Paul's letters revised to their liking**. His followers <u>made their revisions to support and reflect their doctrines</u>. Ultimately, these Marcionian revisions reflected their private interpretations, and what is worse, ***these perversions have survived in some of the ancient Greek New Testament manuscripts*** and account for the differences between the eclectic Critical Greek text and the Textus Receptus.

An early preacher, Irenaeus (c. 115-202 A.D.) points out that "***Marcion cut up that Gospel According to Luke***" (Irenaeus' *Against Heresies*, p. 382). This would account for the large number of changes found in varying manuscripts of Luke and the large number of verses that are left out. It is, for example, understandable why the phrase, "***And when he had thus spoken, he shewed them his hands and his feet.***" (**Luke 24:40**) was omitted by Marcion, since <u>he did not believe in the physical resurrection of Jesus but only in a spiritual resurrection</u>. In fact, the apparatus of the United Bible Society's Critical Greek New Testament text points out **that this verse is omitted by both Marcion and Codex D** (United Bible Society, 2nd ed., p. 317). This verse is omitted from the text of the NEB, RSV and the early editions of the NASV. NASV editors have changed more recent editions to show the verse in brackets - [ ], stating "many mss. do not contain this verse." Thus we see that Codex D and the

NASB, NEB and RSV <u>reflect some of the tampering done by Marcion and his followers</u>.

1 Timothy 3:16 is another example of a Gnostic corruption that has made it into many of the modern versions. The verse reads:

> ***"And without controversy great is the mystery of godliness: <u>God was manifest in the flesh</u>, justified in the Spirit, seen of angels, preached unto the Gentiles, believed on in the world, received up into glory."***

The Jehovah's Witnesses have adopted a number of the Gnostic heresies. One example is that <u>Jesus is a created god</u>, NOT God manifest in the flesh. In the Watchtower's ***New World Translation*** **they change "<u>God</u> was manifest in the flesh,"** as it says in **1 Timothy 3:16, to "<u>He</u> was made manifest in flesh."** In the Textus Receptus Greek, which underlies our King James Bible, it reads ψεοϖ *(theos)* (God) <2316> εφανερωψη *(Ephanerothe)* (was manifested/revealed) <5319> (5681) εν (in) <1722> σαρκι *(sarki)* (the flesh) <4561>.

BUT, the Greek text which underlies the Jehovah's Witness NWT followed the corrupted texts, so it reflects their Gnostic heresy about Christ. However, the JW Bible is not the only bible that follows this corruption – SO DO THE NIV, NASB, NRSV, ESV, and perhaps others. They say ***"He"*** instead of **"<u>God</u>,"** thus following the Gnostic corruption which has made its way into the corrupt Alexandrian text line of texts. That is why so many new versions have missing verses or different readings, because they have been translated from a text line that the Gnostics altered.

The same is true of **John 1:18.** In the **King James Bible** it says:

> ***"No man hath seen God at any time; <u>the only begotten Son</u>, which is in the bosom of the Father, he hath declared him."***

However, the Jehovah's Witness NWT reads, "the only-begotten **god**" (Gk. *monogenes theos*). Again, this is because the Greek text of the NWT reads differently from the Textus Receptus Greek text from which the King James Bible was translated – The TR Greek says (Gk. *monogenes heios*) – **"only begotten Son"** The NWT uses a Greek text that was influenced by Gnosticism.

1881 Westcott & Hort followed the Gnostic corruption – θεον ουδεις εωρακεν πωποτε <u>μονογενης θεος</u> (*monogenes* [***only-begotten***] *theos* [***god***]) ο ων εις τον κολπον του πατρος εκεινος εξηγησατο.

1894 Scrivener, which underlies our KJV has it right - θεον ουδεις εωρακεν πωποτε ο <u>μονογενης υιος</u> (*monogenes* [***only-begotten***] *heios* [***son***]) ο ων εις τον κολπον του πατρος εκεινος εξηγησατο

Again, in both of these examples, the NASV, NIV, ESV and others agree with the NWT because, <u>they are both based on the same corrupt Greek text</u>. It is clear that Gnostic false doctrines have influenced the various Western/Alexandrian manuscripts, and as a result of the modern translations using Greek texts based on corrupt Western manuscripts, Gnosticism influences translations today.

Back to the point I was making – We know that *false gospels* and *false letters* were written and circulated while the apostles were still alive. We find evidence of this in **2 Thessalonians 2:2:**

> *"That ye be not soon shaken in mind, or be troubled, neither by spirit, nor by word, nor <u>by letter as from us</u>, as that the day of Christ is at hand."*

It is obvious that someone had written a letter and was circulating it, claiming that it was from the Apostle Paul and other disciples. **Paul says the letter is spurious, a fake, and a fraud.**

Now consider **2 Peter 2:1-3:**

> *"But there were <u>false prophets</u> also among the people, even as there shall be <u>false teachers</u> among you, who privily <u>shall bring in</u> damnable heresies, even denying the Lord that bought them, and bring upon themselves swift destruction. 2 And*

> *many shall follow their pernicious ways; by reason of whom the way of truth shall be evil spoken of. 3 And through covetousness shall they with feigned words make merchandise of you: whose judgment now of a long time lingereth not, and their damnation slumbereth not."*

These false prophets and teachers are said to ***"privily...bring in damnable heresies."*** That is, they secretly introduced spurious (unauthentic, counterfeit or bogus) teachings that were "damnable heresies" or perversion of the truth. They sought to peddle these heresies among believers. These "damnable heresies" were purposefully written into many New Testament manuscripts and circulated. The modern Bible versions of today are translated from the ancient manuscript group corrupted early on, beginning in the days of the apostles.

CHAPTER 4

WHY YOU SHOULD NOT USE THE MODERN BIBLE VERSIONS

Codex Vaticanus is one of those corrupt manuscripts that the modern Bible versions are based on. An example of that corruption can be seen on this leaf in what would be **Hebrews 1:3.** A marginal note reveals that a corrector had erased and substituted a word in what would be verse 3 (there are no verse divisions in ancient Bibles. Those do not appear until 1560 in the Geneva Bible). A second corrector reinserted the original word with this marginal comment: **"Fool and knave, leave the old reading and do not change it."**

(SEE THE PICTURE NEXT PAGE)

Vaticanus is a very heavily corrected and corrupted text!

I believe that we should NOT use Bible versions that are based on corrupt manuscripts! We have been warned! **Matthew 7:15-20** says:

> *"Beware of false prophets, which come to you in sheep's clothing, but inwardly they are ravening wolves.*

(16) <u>*Ye shall know them by their fruits*</u>*. Do men gather grapes of thorns, or figs of thistles? (17) Even so every <u>good tree bringeth forth good fruit; but a corrupt tree bringeth forth evil fruit</u>. (18) <u>A good tree cannot bring forth evil fruit, neither can a corrupt tree bring forth good fruit</u>. (19) Every tree that bringeth not forth good fruit is hewn down, and cast into the fire. (20) Wherefore <u>by their fruits ye shall know them</u>."*

Luke 6:44-49 "For <u>every tree is known by his own fruit</u>. For of thorns men do not gather figs, nor of a bramble bush gather they grapes. 45 A good man out of the good treasure of his heart bringeth forth that which is good; and an evil man out of the evil treasure of his heart bringeth forth that which is evil: for of the abundance of the heart his mouth speaketh. 46 And why call ye me, Lord, Lord, and do not the things which I say? 47 Whosoever cometh to me, and heareth my sayings, and doeth them, I will show you to whom he is like: 48 He is like a man which built an house, and digged deep, and laid the <u>foundation on a rock</u>: and when the flood arose, the stream beat vehemently upon that house, and could not shake it: for it

> *was founded upon a rock. 49 But he that heareth, and doeth not, is like a man that without a foundation <u>built an house upon the earth</u>; against which the stream did beat vehemently, and immediately it fell; and the ruin of that house was great."*

<u>My premise is a simple one</u>: I will demonstrate to you that the ***Modern Bible Versions*** are the evil fruit from a corrupt tree, planted by ***Wolves in Sheep's clothing***, whose plan was and is to confuse the sheep and ultimately destroy their faith in the Word(s) of God, thus getting them to build their lives on the unsure shifting sands of human reason ***instead of*** building their lives on the **SURE FOUNDATION OF GOD'S WORD, the King James Bible, which is accurately translated from the texts that God has preserved. Why is that important?**

For genuine believers, the Bible is the foundation of literally every **doctrine**, **belief** and **practice** in New Testament Christianity! If a belief, principle or practice does not have a biblical base it should be rejected. We read in **1 Thessalonians 5:21** ***"Prove all things; hold fast that which is good."*** The English word ***prove*** is a translation of the Greek word dokimazete – δοκιμαζετε (*dok-im-ad'zate*). The word carries the idea of ***proving a thing whether it is worthy or not***. So, the question is, <u>how are we to</u>

go about ***proving*** something? I believe **Isaiah 8:20** gives us insight into the answer to this question – *"To the law and to the testimony: <u>if they speak not according to this word</u>, it is because there is no light in them."* In other words, **examine everything by the words of the Bible** and if it does not line up, reject it!

It should be obvious to you that I believe in the Verbal Plenary Inspiration for the 66 books of the Bible and I also believe in the Verbal Plenary preservation of those same 66 books! I believe that the process of God breathing out His Words occurred only once when He breathed out or 'inspired' the Hebrew, Aramaic and Greek texts. Though the process of inspiration has never been repeated, the product of inspiration, that is, the Hebrew, Aramaic, and Greek Words, have been preserved by God in the Words of the Masoretic Hebrew and Textus Receptus (traditional) Greek that underlie the King James Bible.

I assert that we DO have the words of God today and that our King James Bible is the best translation of those preserved words. There has been none better, there is none better, there will be none better in the future.

Now here is the problem. **If** the Bible was not inspired, then it CANNOT be used as a reliable standard! **If** the Bible was inspired and the readings lost, then it CANNOT be used as a reliable standard! And lastly, **if** the Bible texts are not preserved, then it CANNOT be used as a reliable standard!

That is the belief and teaching of those who laid the foundation of the modern Bible versions. They do not believe God has preserved His Words and therefore the Bible is **NOT** a reliable standard! They adopted the ***higher critical*** view of the Bible. But that is **NOT** what I believe!

SO WHAT IS "HIGHER CRITICISM?"

As I explained previously, **higher criticism treats the Bible as a text created by human beings** at a particular historical time and for various human motives. "They based their interpretations on a presupposition that the Bible is not divinely inspired and that a conglomerate of unknown authors and editors assembled and modified the Bible as they desired."
(www.foundationsforfreedom.net/Topics/Bible/Bible_Reliability.html).

BRIEF OVERVIEW OF THE MOTLEY CREW BEHIND THE MODERN BIBLE VERSIONS

There are many men who undermined the authority of the Scriptures by denying its divine inspiration and preservation and promoting what we call textual criticism.

If you were to take the time to look into those who have laid the foundation for the modern Bible versions, you would understand the title of this section. You would find a group of doubters, deceivers, skeptics, occultists, heretics, unbelievers and more. I do not have the time in this series to thoroughly expose the beliefs, teaching and practices of these men; however, I will name some of the key players in this *motley crew* and make brief comments about their beliefs.

RICHARD SIMON

Richard Simon (1638-1712) is often called *the Father of Biblical Criticism.*
(www.1902encyclopedia.com/S/SIM/richard-simon.html).

He was a French Roman Catholic who held apostate and heretical views that undermined the authority and preservation of the Word(s) of God. For instance, he believed there were men before Adam. He rejected the Bible as the sole authority for faith and practice and held that Catholic tradition was of equal authority with the Bible. However, his revolutionary apostasy was his contention "that **<u>no original text of the Bible exists</u>**, that the texts one possesses have developed and have been altered through the ages, and that it is therefore necessary to apply the method of critical evaluation to biblical materials to establish the most accurate human form of the revelation. This method involves philology (study of texts and trying to

reconstruct them), textual study, historical researches, and comparative studies."
(www.bookrags.com/research/simon-richard-16381712-eoph)

This is a key building block undermining the preservation of the Word and Words of God. He published numerous books supporting his apostate teachings including *his 1689 Critical History of the Text of the New Testament* that advances the idea that the Scripture has not been carefully preserved and therefore the Bible cannot be entirely authoritative. Previous to that volume, he published one called *Critical History of the Old Testament* where he denied Moses was the author of the Pentateuch. Further, he stated that the Old Testament is a mixture of truth and myth. In 1702 he published a four volume New Testament based on the Latin Vulgate, but it included variant readings from the Greek and critical remarks.

JOHANN SALOMO SEMLER

JOHANN SALOMO SEMLER (1725-1791) is sometimes called the *Father of German Rationalism.* **Rationalism** is basically the theory that human reason is the best guide for belief and actions. It is the theory that the exercise of reason, rather than experience, authority, or spiritual revelation, provides the primary basis for knowledge and truth. "He rejected the deity of Jesus Christ and believed that revelation must be judged by human reason. The sophisticated mind should have no obligation to believe what is 'unreasonable' in the Bible." (http://history-perspective.com/critical_theories.html).

The common thread is that Semler was strongly influenced by Richard Simon, and particularly his 1689 book, *Critical History.* More important to the focus of this message, Semler is *The Father of the Recension Theory*. This theory claims that the Received text is an editorial recension created centuries after the apostles. Additionally, the textual readings favoring theological orthodoxy should be suspect. Why? Because he denied biblical preservation and falsely believed the orthodox readings were created by textual editors during the early centuries. Because of this view, he taught other manuscripts, particularly the older ones, which shortens the passage or leaves it out, should be followed.

I should also point out that Semler began grouping manuscripts into three families: Alexandrian (Egyptian), Western and Asiatic (Byzantine). He believed the Alexandrian was superior to the Byzantine.

As an aside, Semler became a believer in alchemy, whereby ordinary metals are converted into gold. Tragically, what he managed to do was convert the Gold of the Word of God into dirt of doubt.

JOHANN JAKOB GRIESBACH

JOHANN JAKOB GRIESBACH (1745-1812). He adopted Selmer's recension theory that claimed that the Received Text was an editorial revision created centuries after the apostles. This myth, as you well know, was later popularized by Westcott and Hort.

Tartu University Library   hdl: 10062/2038

J. J. Griesbach was <u>one of the earliest fathers of modern textual criticism</u>. Marvin R. Vincet says in his book *A History of the Textual Criticism of the New Testament*, published in 1899, "With Griesbach, really critical texts may be said to have begun."

The late Bruce Metzger said, "Griesbach laid the foundations for all subsequent work on the Greek text of the New Testament." He further asserted, "the importance of Griesbach for New Testament textual criticism can scarcely be overestimated." (Metzger, *The Text of the New Testament*) He rejected the deity of Jesus Christ and the supernatural infallibility of Holy Scripture. **Griesbach was the <u>first to declare</u>**

<u>Mark 16:9-20 spurious</u>. He omitted it from the 1796 edition of his critical Greek New Testament.

I own a copy of his 1809 American critical edition of his Greek New Testament. It was published by Harvard College. They published this edition because it was "a most powerful weapon to be used against the supporters of verbal inspiration." (Theodore Letis, *The Ecclesiastical Text*) This was done around the same time that Harvard College gave way to Unitarianism.

Here is the point: The enemies of the inspiration of the Bible clearly understood that, in general, modern textual criticism, and specifically Griesbach's critical New Testament, weakened the key doctrines of the Christian faith (such as inspiration, preservation, etc.) and undermines the authority of the Bible.

KARL LACHMANN

KARL LACHMANN (1793-1851) was not even a Bible scholar but a professor of Classical and German Philology at Berlin. He has been described as a German rationalist [human reason is the sole source and final test of all truth]. Lachmann's theory and belief was that all of the extant New Testament manuscripts were corrupt and that it is not possible to dogmatically reconstruct the apostolic text. His goal was to secure the text that was in widest use in the 4th Century, the time of Jerome, and he referenced the Alexandrian manuscripts and the writings of Origin and others. Lachmann did not study the New Testament as the supernaturally-inspired and divinely-preserved Word of God, but as a mere book. He was a profane man who treated the Bible like any other book and his textual research was a mere scholarly venture. He began to apply the same rules that he had used in editing texts of the Greek classics to the N.T. Greek text because he presupposed it was hopelessly corrupted. His theory undermined the doctrine of divine preservation by claiming that the apostolic text cannot possibly be known for certain and the best that could be done was to rediscover the 4th century text.

BROOKE FOSS WESTCOTT AND JOHN ANTHONY HORT

Brooke Foss Westcott (January 12, 1825 – July 27, 1901) (pictured at the left) and **John Anthony Hort** (1828-1892) (pictured right).

They are the **Fathers of the Modern Bible Versions**. They got many of their ideas from Griesbach and Lachmann. Westcott and Hort built their own critical Greek New Testament text based primarily on two conflicting Greek uncial MSS – Codex Vaticanus and Codex Sinaiticus. These perverted MSS do not even agree among themselves. In the Gospels alone they differ in over 3,000 places. The ironic thing is that Westcott and Hort knew this when they created their text! <u>Virtually all the modern versions are based on Westcott and Hort's critical Greek New Testament</u>. In the introduction to the 24th edition of Nestle's Greek New Testament, editors Erwin Nestle and Kurt Aland make the following admission: "Thus **THE TEXT, BUILT UPON THE WORK OF THE 19TH CENTURY, HAS REMAINED AS A WHOLE UNCHANGED**, particularly since the research of recent years has not yet led to the establishment of a generally acknowledged N.T. text" (Erwin Nestle and Kurt Aland, *Novum Testamentum Graece*, 24th edition, 1960, p. 62).

EUGENE NIDA

EUGENE NIDA was born in Oklahoma in 1914. He has the dubious distinction of being the father of the **heretical dynamic equivalency theory** of Bible translation that is used in almost all of the modern Bible versions. He believes the record of Jacob wrestling with the Angel was not a literal event. He denies the substitutionary blood atonement of Christ (Nida, *Theory and Practice*, 1969, p. 53). He denies that Christ died to satisfy God's justice. He believes the blood of the cross was merely symbolic of Christ's death and is never used in the Bible "in the sense of propitiation." He retired from being the Executive Secretary for Translations for the American Bible Society in 1980. Today he lives in Brussels, Belgium.

KURT ALAND

KURT ALAND (March 28, 1915-April 13, 1994) of the Nestle-Aland Greek New Testament fame, denied the verbal inspiration of the Bible and wanted to see all denominations united into one "body" by the acceptance of a new ecumenical canon of Scripture which would take into account the Catholic apocryphal books (*The Problem of the New Testament Canon*, pp. 6,7,30-33).

BRUCE MANNING METZGER

<u>BRUCE MANNING METZGER</u> (February 9, 1914 – February 13, 2007). He edited and provided commentary for many Bible translations and wrote dozens of books. He was one of the editors of the <u>United Bible Societies'</u> standard Greek New Testament, **the starting point for nearly all translations of the New Testament in recent decades**. In 1952, he became a contributor to the <u>Revised Standard Version</u> (RSV) of the Bible, and became general editor of the *Reader's Digest Bible* (a condensed version of the RSV) in 1982. From 1977 to 1990, he also chaired the Committee on Translators for the <u>New Revised Standard Version</u> (NRSV) of the Bible, which included the Apocrypha.

WHAT METZGER BELIEVED

Metzger believed the Old Testament was a "matrix (compilation) of myth, legend, and history." (Note: Jesus affirmed the Old Testament's authenticity Luke 24:44-45)

Metzger did not believe that Moses wrote the Pentateuch but that "the Pentateuch took shape over a long period of time." (Note: **Jesus affirmed that Moses wrote it – John 7:19; Matthew 8:4; John 5:46**).

Metzger did not believe in the biblical worldwide flood. (Note: **Jesus affirmed the global flood – Matthew 24:37-39**)

Metzger believed the book of Job is a folktale.

Metzger believed Isaiah was written by Isaiah plus two or three unknown men who wrote centuries later. (Note: **Jesus affirmed that Isaiah wrote the book that carries his name – Luke 3:4**).

Metzger believed that Jonah was a "didactic narrative [story intended to teach a lesson] which has taken older material from the realm of **popular legend** and put it to a new, more consequential use." (Note: **Jesus affirmed that Jonah was real – Matthew 12:39-41**).

Metzger believed that Paul did not write the Pastoral Epistles [1 & 2 Timothy and Titus]. **1 Timothy 1:1** says he did. **2 Timothy 1:1** says he did. **Titus 1:1** says he did!

What puzzles me is that Metzger is adored by modern day Bible scholars, theologians, preachers, students and even many fundamental Baptists. I concur with Dr. Jeffrey Khoo who said – **"True and faithful Biblicists ought to be warned that Metzger's scholarship is not one to be desired nor admired."** Christian friend, "Metzger's philosophy and methodology will only lead to chronic uncertainty and perpetual unbelief of the total inspiration and perfect preservation of the Holy Scriptures." **James 3:11-12:**

> ***"Doth a fountain send forth at the same place sweet water and bitter? (12) Can the fig tree, my brethren, bear olive berries? either a vine, figs? so can no fountain both yield salt water and fresh."***

CHAPTER 5

CONCLUSION

These men characterized in the last chapter were all apostates! There is not a believer in the bunch. These are indeed a motley crew, each contributing a wide variety of apostate and heretical ideas that undermine the Word(s) of God. These are the men behind the modern versions!

THINGS THAT ARE DIFFERENT ARE NOT THE SAME!

I believe that if I showed you an apple and an orange and asked you, "are these the same or different," you would say "they are different." While they certainly are both in the fruit family, they are different!

If I held up an axe and a chain saw and asked you if they were different or the same, I believe you would say, "they are different." While they are both used to cut wood, they are different.

If I held up a United States One Dollar Bill and United States One Hundred Dollar Bill and asked you if they were different or the same, you would surely say, "they are different." While they are both legal tender for all debts public and private, I believe everyone would rather have a $100 bill than a $1 bill.

Yet, when it comes to the differences in Bible versions, we are being told that there are not that many differences, and that even the differences there are, really do not affect any major doctrines. Therefore it really does not matter! **I DISAGREE!** Why? Because, **THINGS THAT ARE DIFFERENT ARE NOT THE SAME!**

As I have been pointing out in this series, there are two VERY DIFFERENT Greek text streams from which the New Testament has been translated. The Tyndale, Matthews, Great, Geneva and King James New Testaments have all been translated from the Eastern, Antiochian, Traditional, Received or Textus Receptus text group (all names for the same text group). There are <u>more than 5,000</u> Greek manuscripts and portions in this group. On the other hand, the Modern Bible Versions are translated from the Western, Alexandrian or Minority text group (all names for the same text group). There are <u>about 45</u> manuscripts or portions in this group.

DR. JACK MOORMAN OF LONDON, ENGLAND, WHO I PERSONALLY KNOW AND HAVE ATTENDED HIS CHURCH, HAS PUBLISHED A BOOK THAT LISTS THE 8,000 DIFFERENCES

BETWEEN THE NEW TESTAMENT GREEK WORDS OF THE TEXTUS RECEPTUS UNDERLYING THE KING JAMES NEW TESTAMENT AND THE WORDS OF NESTLES-ALAND'S 26TH & 27TH GREEK NEW TESTAMENT WHICH UNDERLIES THE MODERN BIBLE VERSIONS.

IT IS AVAILABLE HERE WITH SAMPLE PAGES AND LINKS TO DISTRIBUTORS: Jack A. Moorman Books (theoldpathspublications.com)

Christian friends, **THINGS THAT ARE DIFFERENT ARE NOT THE SAME!** 8,000 differences should prove that point! In the chart below, I want to point out the **17 verses** that are completely missing from many of the Modern Bible Versions.

17 Verses Completely Missing From the Modern Bible Versions

King **J**ames **B**ible Compared to the **N**ew **I**nternational **V**ersion & the **E**nglish **S**tandard **V**ersion

Major Verse Discrepancies between KJV, NIV & ESV

(SEE CHART NEXT PAGE)

Verses Completely Omitted From Two of the Most Popular Modern Versions

King James Version	New International Version	English Standard Version
Matthew 17:21	Entire Verse Omitted	Entire Verse Omitted
Matthew 18:11	Entire Verse Omitted	Entire Verse Omitted
Matthew 23:14	Entire Verse Omitted	Entire Verse Omitted
Mark 7:16	Entire Verse Omitted	Entire Verse Omitted
Mark 9:44	Entire Verse Omitted	Entire Verse Omitted
Mark 9:46	Entire Verse Omitted	Entire Verse Omitted
Mark 11:26	Entire Verse Omitted	Entire Verse Omitted
Mark 15:28	Entire Verse Omitted	Entire Verse Omitted
Luke 17:36	Entire Verse Omitted	Entire Verse Omitted
Luke 23:17	Entire Verse Omitted	Entire Verse Omitted
John 5:4	Entire Verse Omitted	Entire Verse Omitted
Acts 8:37	Entire Verse Omitted	Entire Verse Omitted
Acts 15:34	Entire Verse Omitted	Entire Verse Omitted
Acts 24:7	Entire Verse Omitted	Entire Verse Omitted
Acts 28:29	Entire Verse Omitted	Entire Verse Omitted
Romans 16:24	Entire Verse Omitted	Entire Verse Omitted
1 John 5:7 (KJV) For there are three that bear record <u>in heaven, the Father, the Word, and the</u>	**1 John 5: 7 (NIV)** For there are three that testify: [omit – **in heaven, the Father, the Word, and the**	**1 John 5:7 (ESV)** For there are three that testify: [omit – **in heaven, the Father, the Word, and the**

Holy Ghost: and these three are one. 8 And there are three that bear witness in earth, the Spirit, and the water, and the blood: and these three agree in one.	Holy Ghost: and these three are one.] 8 the Spirit, the water and the blood; and the three are in agreement.	Holy Ghost: and these three are one.] 8 the Spirit and the water and the blood; and these three agree.

JOHANNINE COMMA

I John 5:7-8 is called the *Johannine comma*. It lends strong support to the Triune nature of God! Bruce Metzger, one of **The Motley Crew** behind the modern Bible versions, wrote in his 1992 book *The Test of the New Testament: Its Transmission, Corruption, and Restoration* on page 62 that the "the first Greek manuscript discovered which contained the passage relating to the *Three Heavenly Witnesses* of **I John 5:7-8** was a New Testament from the late 15th or early 16th century." That is just NOT TRUE! There is an abundance of other ancient manuscript evidence in support of the passage. As Edward Hills says, "The first undisputed citations of the *Johannine comma* occur in the writing of two 4th-century Spanish bishops... In the 5th century the *Johannine comma* was quoted by several orthodox African writers to defend the doctrine of the Trinity against the gainsaying of the Vandals, who...were fanatically attached to the Arian heresy." Evidence for the early existence of the *Johannine comma* is found in the Latin versions and in the writings of the Latin Church Fathers." Among these is

Cyprian (c. 250) and Cassiodorus (480–570), as well as an Old Latin manuscript of the 5th or 6th century, and in the *Speculum*, a treatise which contains an Old Latin text.

I stand aligned with those who believe that it is very probable Origen (c. 185-254 A.D.), the great corrupter of the Bible, is responsible for removing **1 John 5:7**. Without **1 John 5:7** the Greek syntax of verses 6-8 makes no sense.

(For a thorough discussion of the Johannine Comma, see Michael Maynard Books (theoldpathspublications.com)

Now we move on to the issue of **Mark 1:2-3**. This passage in Mark is an important one because it demonstrates that the underlying text of the King James Bible is the one God has preserved. The KJV correctly says, "it is written by the prophets!" The passage quotes two prophets, Malachi and Isaiah.

Mark 1:2-3 (KJV)	**Mark 1:2-3 (NIV)**	**Mark 1:2-3 (ESV)**
As it is written in the prophets, Behold, I send my messenger before thy face, which shall prepare thy way before thee. The voice of one crying in the wilderness, Prepare ye the way of the Lord, make his paths straight.	It is written in Isaiah the prophet: "I will send my messenger ahead of you, who will prepare your way, a voice of one calling in the desert, 'Prepare the way for the Lord, make straight paths for him.'	As it is written in Isaiah the prophet "Behold, I send my messenger before your face, who will prepare your way the voice of one crying in the wilderness: 'Prepare the way of the Lord, make his paths straight,'"

> *Malachi 3:1 (KJV) Behold, <u>I will send my messenger, and he shall prepare the way before me</u>: and the LORD, whom ye seek, shall suddenly come to his temple, even the messenger of the covenant, whom ye delight in: behold, he shall come, saith the LORD of hosts.*

> *Isaiah 40:3 (KJV) The voice of him that crieth in the wilderness, Prepare ye the way of the LORD, make straight in the desert a highway for our God.*

The King James Bible correctly states, it is written by the **prophets** **NOT** just by Isaiah the prophet.

There are thousands of other missing phrases, and words in the NIV and ESV. I want to give you some more examples. The NIV and ESV claim that **John 7:53-8:11** are missing in "the earliest and most reliable manuscripts." It is the account of the woman taken in adultery. However, they do not tell you that this passage is designated as the *Pericope De Adultera,* referring to the woman caught in the act of adultery, and is included in numerous uncials such as D05, G, H, K, M, U, and G. Among the minuscule or cursive manuscripts it is in 28, 700, 892, 1009, 1010, 1071, 1079, 1195, 1216, 1344, 1365, 1546, 1646, 2148, and 2174. <u>Most Greek manuscripts contain this passage</u>. It also is in early translations such as the Bohairic Coptic

Version, the Syriac Palestinian Version and the Ethiopic Version, all of which date from the second to the sixth centuries. It is clearly the reading of the majority of the Old Latin manuscripts and Jerome's Latin Vulgate. The passage has patristic support: Didascalia (third century), Ambrosiaster (fourth century), Ambrose (fourth century), the Apostolic Constitutions (which are the largest liturgical collections of writings from Antioch Syria in about 380 AD), Jerome (420 AD), and Augustine (430 AD). [Dr. Thomas Holland's *Crowned With Glory*].

Two final illustrations of the thousands to choose from...

Matthew 5:44 (KJV) But I say unto you, Love your enemies, bless them that curse you, <u>do good to them that hate you, and pray for them which despitefully use you, and persecute you;</u>	Matthew 5:44 (NIV) But I tell you: Love your enemies and pray for those who persecute you, [More than half the verse is omitted]	Matthew 5:44 (ESV) – But I say to you, Love your enemies and pray for those who persecute you, [More than half the verse is omitted]
Mark 6:11 (KJV) – And whosoever shall not receive you, nor hear you, when ye depart thence, shake off the dust under your feet for a testimony against them. Verily I say unto you, It shall be more tolerable for Sodom and Gomorrha in the day of judgment, than for that city.	Mark 6:11 (NIV) And if any place will not welcome you or listen to you, shake the dust off your feet when you leave, as a testimony against them." [A third of the verse is missing]	Mark 6:11 (ESV)– And if any place will not receive you and they will not listen to you, when you leave, shake off the dust that is on your feet as a testimony against them. [The last third of the verse is missing]

Christian friends, I have shared this to make it clear that *Things That Are Different Are Not The Same!* Remember, there are 8,000 (perhaps more) differences between the underlying Greek text of the King James Bible and the Modern Versions. I close with **Deuteronomy 4:2:**

"Ye shall not add unto the word which I command you, neither shall ye diminish ought from it, that ye may keep the commandments of the LORD your God which I command you."

CONTRASTING VIEWS OF THE SCRIPTURES: THE VIEW OF THE CRITICS & THE VIEW OF CHRIST

Matthew 7:17-20 "Even so every good tree bringeth forth good fruit; but a corrupt tree bringeth forth evil fruit. 18 A good tree cannot bring forth evil fruit, neither can a corrupt tree bring forth good fruit. 19 Every tree that bringeth not forth good fruit is hewn down, and cast into the fire. 20 Wherefore by their fruits ye shall know them."

I have pointed out how the New Testament autographs came under attack almost before the ink was dry. There were those in the times of the apostles who corrupted the Word of God (**2 Corinthians 2:17**). Further, false Gospels and false letters were circulated, which claimed they were authentic (**2 Thessalonians 2:2**). In **2 Corinthians 4:1-2** the Apostle Paul wrote — *"Therefore seeing we have this* *ministry, as we have received mercy, we faint not; 2 But have renounced the hidden things of dishonesty, not walking in craftiness, nor* <u>*handling the word of God deceitfully*</u>*; but by manifestation of the truth commending ourselves to every man's conscience in the sight of God."* In this verse Paul writes that he and his companions are not like others that were **"handling the word of God deceitfully."** The phrase means, <u>they had not corrupted God's Words with error</u>! We know that there were false teachers and preachers who were introducing "damnable heresies" in their teachings and then amended the Gospels and letters to support their teachings and circulated those corrupted writings. In the days of the apostles, and shortly afterwards, numerous false teachings and heresies were being advocated, among them Nicolaitianism, Gnosticism, Arianism, Donatism, Pelagianism, Neo-Platonism and others.

Jude wrote to the believers of his day (65-67 A.D.) that they need to *"earnestly contend for the faith once delivered to the saints"* because deceitful, ungodly men were changing the nature of the New Testament teaching on grace and salvation! (**Jude 1:3-4**). These false doctrines influenced the transmission of Scripture and account for some of the differences in the line of manuscripts.

CONTRASTING VIEWS OF THE SCRIPTURES

How do the beliefs of Jesus Christ compare to the beliefs of those who produced the *critical text*, which underlies almost all of the modern versions of the Bible?

In any study of the Bible versions' controversy, there are two names that you will come across regularly – **Westcott and Hort**. Many consider them the **fathers of modern textual criticism**. So, let's begin by telling you something about them and their beliefs.

BROOKE FOSS WESTCOTT AND FENTON JOHN ANTHONY HORT

Brooke Foss Westcott (1825-1901) **and Fenton John Anthony Hort** (1828-1892) produced a Greek New Testament in 1881 based on Codex Vaticanus from the Vatican and the findings of Constantine Tischendorf, Codex Sinaiticus. I visited St. Catherine's Monastery in 2008. St. Catherine's Monastery is historically significant in the textual controversy because it is there that Tischendorf discovered leaves of Codex Sinaiticus in a trash can, ready to be burned.

The **critical Greek New Testament** produced by Westcott and Hort was the basis for the Revised Version (RV), also called the English Revised Version

(ERV). The New Testament came out in 1881. The American Standard Version (ASV) was the American edition of this work. Further, Westcott and Hort developed a theory of textual criticism which underlies their Greek New Testament and several other Greek New Testaments (such as the Nestle's text and the United Bible Society's text). Greek New Testaments such as these produced the modern English translations of the Bible we have today. So it is important for us to know what Westcott and Hort believed because they have so greatly influenced modern textual criticism and the modern versions of the Bible.

BELIEFS OF WESTCOTT & HORT

Hort clearly <u>believed in the new theory of evolution</u>. He wrote to the Rev. John Ellerton, April 3, 1860: "But the book which has most engaged me is Darwin. Whatever may be thought of it, it is a book that one is proud to be contemporary with. . . . My feeling is strong that the theory is unanswerable. If so, it opens up a new period." (Hort, *Life of Hort*, I:416).

Westcott did <u>not believe in the literal interpretation of the creation account of Genesis</u>. Westcott wrote to the Archbishop of Canterbury on Old Testament criticism, March 4, 1890: "No one now, I suppose, holds that the first three chapters of Genesis, for example, give a literal history—I could never understand how anyone reading them with open eyes could think they did." (Westcott, *Life of Westcott*, II:69).

Westcott wrote concerning the Scriptures – "I reject the word infallibility of Holy Scriptures over-whelmingly." (Westcott, *The Life and Letters of Brooke Foss Westcott*, Vol. I, p.207).

Dr. Wilbur Pickering writes that, **Hort did not hold to a high view of inspiration.** (*The Identity of the New Testament Text*, p.212).

Westcott believed in Salvation by Baptism! He wrote in a letter – **"by baptism he may if he will, truly live forever.** I do not say that Baptism is absolutely necessary, though from the word of the Scriptures I can see no exception, but I do not think we have a right to exclaim against the idea of the commencement of a spiritual life, **conditionally from Baptism,** any more than we have to deny the commencement of a moral life from birth." (www.workmenforchrist.org/Bible/History/Westcott.html).

Westcott did not believe in a literal Heaven or a literal Hell. He believed Heaven was a state of mind and said so – "heaven is a state and not a place." *and* "(Hell is) not the place of punishment of the guilty, (it is) the common abode of departed spirits."

Westcott did not believe in the miracles recorded in the Bible. He said, "I never read an account of a miracle but I seem instinctively to feel its improbability, and discover somewhat of evidence in the account of it."

Hort said – "The fact is, I do not see how God's justice can be satisfied without every man's suffering in his own person the full penalty for his sins."

Hort believed in the meritorious works of the sacraments. He wrote, "we dare not forsake the Sacraments, or God will forsake us." He further said, "I wish we were more agreed on the doctrinal part; but you know I am a staunch sacerdotalist, and there is not much profit in arguing about first principles."

A whole book could be written (and has been for that matter) on the unbiblical and heretical views of Westcott & Hort. What I want to point out is this. Our Lord says:

> *"A good tree cannot bring forth evil fruit, <u>neither can a corrupt tree bring forth good fruit.</u> Wherefore by their fruits ye shall know them." Matthew 7:18, 20.*

It is clear to me that a corrupt tree cannot produce good fruit! Since the modern versions have at their primary root the critical text produced by Westcott & Hort, it follows that these Bibles will be corrupt also!

I suggest you follow Jesus Christ and His views of the Scripture.

HOW DID JESUS VIEW THE SCRIPTURES?

Jesus never involved Himself in higher or lower criticism nor attempted to recover the original autographs. He never corrected or criticized Scripture, even though He did not possess the original autographs. Rather He said:

"Sanctify them through thy truth: thy word is truth." John 17:17

- **Jesus** accepted the Old Testament Jewish canon, but rejected the Apocrypha (**Luke 24:44**)

- **Jesus** taught that every word of Scripture proceeded from God (**Matthew 4:4**)

- **Jesus** taught the doctrine of the preservation of Scripture (**Matthew 5:17-18; 24:35; Luke 6:17**)

- **Jesus** taught that the Old Testament Scriptures pointed to Him (**Luke 24:27, 44**)

- **Jesus** taught that man will be judged by God's Word (**John 12:47-48**)

- **Jesus** taught the absolute authority of Scripture (**John 10:34-36**)

- **Jesus** pre-authenticated the New Testament writings as Scripture (**John 14:26; 16:12-13**)

- **Jesus believed** in the Genesis account of creation (**Matthew 19:4-6; Mark 10:6-8**)

- **Jesus believed** in the Mosaic authorship of the Pentateuch (**Matthew 8:4; John 5:46; 7:19**)

- **Jesus believed** in the historicity and universality of the Noahic Flood (**Matthew 24:37-39**)

- **Jesus believed** in the historicity of Abraham (**John 8:56**)

- **Jesus believed** in the historicity of Sodom and Gomorrah (**Matthew 10:15; 11:23-24**)

- **Jesus believed** Lot's wife was turned into a pillar of salt (**Luke 17:32**)

- **Jesus believed** God gave manna from heaven to Israel (**John 6:31, 49, 58**)

- **Jesus believed** in the Davidic authorship of the Psalms (**Matthew 22:43**)

- **Jesus believed** in the historicity of Jonah and the whale (**Matthew 12:39-41**)

- **Jesus believed** in the Danielic authorship of Daniel (**Matthew 24:15**)

- **Jesus believed** in the unity of the book of Isaiah (**Matthew 13:14-15; Mark 7:6; John 12:38-41**)

- **Jesus believed** the Jews had a history of rejecting God's Word (**Luke 11:47-51**) [this section adapted from an article by John A. Kohler, III]

Westcott, Hort, Nestle, Aland, Metzger and other modern critics reject the position our Lord held on the Scriptures. I urge you to reject the fruit of these critics, the Modern Bible Versions produced from their works, and **take the position of the Lord Jesus Christ**. If you will do that, that will narrow your choices down to the New Testament of Tyndale, the Geneva Bible or the King James Bible. ***The CREAM OF THE CROP IS OUR KING JAMES BIBLE!*** That is why we use it. That is why you should use it as well.

ABOUT THE AUTHOR

David L. Brown was born in Michigan. He came to know Christ as his Savior as the result of a Sunday school teacher throwing away the liberal curriculum, teaching through the book of Romans, and sharing the Gospel. He has been married to Linda for 53 years. She was a young lady from his home church.

David attended a Michigan University then transferred to a Christian University and Seminary where he completed a Bachelor's Degree in Social Science and Theology. He holds a Master's Degree in Theology, and Ph.D. in History, specializing in the history of the English Bible.

Since December 1979, he has been the Pastor of the First Baptist Church of Oak Creek, Wisconsin (an independent, fundamental, Baptist Church using the King James Bible and conservative music). Previous to that, he pastored an independent Baptist Church in

Michigan for five years, was an assistant pastor for 4 years, and served with his wife as short term missionaries in Haiti.

Dr. Brown is the president of the ***King James Bible Research Council,***

(www.kjbrc.org),

an organization dedicated to promoting the King James Bible and its underlying texts and other traditional text translations around the world in a solid and sensible way.

He is also the president of ***Logos Communication Consortium, Inc.*** (www.logosresourcepages.org), a research organization that produces a large variety of materials warning Christians of present dangers in our culture.

Dr. Brown is the Curator of the ***Biblical Heritage Archives*** and regularly takes his rare Bible, manuscript and artifact collection to fundamental Baptist Churches teaching and preaching on the history of our English Bible, showing how God has preserved His Word(s), and why we should use the King James Bible.

He also serves as a consultant for individuals, museums, colleges, universities, and seminaries that desire to acquire or have collections of biblical manuscripts and Bibles. He is an antiquarian book dealer with contacts around the world.

He is the author of many books and articles. Many can be found here with links and sample pages:

Brown Books (theoldpathspublications.com)

He can be contacted at:
>**Dr. David L. Brown**
>**P. O. Box 173**
>**Oak Creek, WI. 53154**
>**Phone: 414-768-9754**
>**Email: PastorDavidLBrown@gmail.com**

www.ingramcontent.com/pod-product-compliance
Lightning Source LLC
Chambersburg PA
CBHW061349140726
47997CB00003B/1118